Talking About Golf

TALKING
ABOUT
GOLF

poems by

DARYL J. LUKAS

ACKNOWLEDGMENTS

We would like to thank Finishing Line Press and
Shadows Ink Publications for publishing the following
chapbooks in which many of these poems first appeared:

Ode to Toledo (Finishing Line Press: 2006,)
Two Guys Talking at the Four Horsemen (Shadows
Ink Publications: 2007) and *The Hotel Victory*
(Shadows Ink Publications: 2009.)

Some of the poems have been modified.

Library of Congress Control Number: 2013904402

ISBN: 978-0-615-77324-7

Printed in the United States by Morris Publishing®
3212 East Highway 30
Kearney, NE 68847
1-800-650-7888

for Diane

Contents

II. THE SCHOOLHOUSE

III. TIGER STADIUM

IV. HARWELL'S VOICE

Talking About Golf

I. WHEN I CAME BACK DYING

When I Came Back Dying

The house was sitting empty, television on,
when a narrator, describing the death of Paul Cezanne,
said *after painting one day, he came back dying*;
while a blank page was patiently waiting
for my unexpected verb, for the nouns to somehow
become a perfect alchemy of words,
to come trudging in through the newly laid snow
with their tiny footprints searching for
the tilting branches of the trees, or
a cool clean northern breeze,
or someone kneeling beside a headstone,
as an anonymous voice continued to recognize
the beauty of an artist's work.

I realized then, that everything is words,
either said or unsaid, printed or otherwise written,
while still trudging along searching for that feeling
of complete satisfaction within, if only once,
now conscious of one's own mortality
and hoping to stumble upon Jesus
in the happenstance of a poem.

But only later did I realize, that it was actually
a premonition of me when I came back dying
to an unfinished sentence,
making just the slightest impression
on an underlying page.

Nine Miles to Trenton

Everything is at stake.
- George Washington (1776)

Your only journal entry on that Christmas Day, now pre-
ordained, with the fate of unborn millions depending upon
God and your suicidal plan. Knowing full well that come the
thirty-first, but for your gritty little handful, they would not
re-enlist, so weary after suffering so many defeats

and the latest of pell-mell retreats
through New York and New Jersey
and finally to safety on this west bank
of the Delaware.

Even you, just one week earlier
suggesting *the game is pretty near up*
when writing your brother and then your wife

discussing interior decoration
and what crops to be planted next season
and the breath-taking vistas at Mount Vernon

when divine intervention or the sheer insanity of desperation
took hold, though really not a choice with so few options, but
still, with so very much to lose, your last name having already
been mutinied, ripped to shreds, like so many near-misses
through your overcoat.

But now, standing stalwart in your resolution and once more
tempting fate, while leading your soldiers through the freezing
cold, with their brutal exhaustion beyond comprehension
but for you, *statuesque* when crossing.

Two Guys Talking at the Four Horsemen Tavern

Late afternoon eavesdropping,
when the lacquered mahogany begins to pool
circles of residue forming islands
within the well-worn grooves,
the half-filled ash trays and half-empty glasses of beer
just a spurious correlation
as two rumpled shirts sitting in the corner,
one a gray flannel, toasted each other,
their aberrant conversation muffled
by the normal weekday chatter, like
the irritating strike zone flickering on the television
with their octaves being pitched both above and below.

But something about family and old friends
and thoughts becoming scattered, then I heard
"He knew my face, he said I looked familiar
like someone he used to know,"
and then a few more moments passed
before the man without flannel simply asked,
"Has he lost a lot of weight?"
His question hanged there, like smoke,
just sitting there without an answer,
when the other man finally said,
"He doesn't even know that he's sick;
he still thinks he's at home."

Then they toasted again,
a broken promise,
to remain always young.

Rules of Engagement

I begin watching, simultaneously at first,
with the pick-up game of football becoming
a more welcomed substitute for the world news,
always in or about some far away land,
being perhaps, not so far away at all,
what with the same caveats or pretenses
when telling their truths, and tensions rising.
So gradually, the endless droning about China
and North Korea and Syria and Iran …
disappears, no longer matters
(fading into the background)
as I slowly ascertain the boundaries
of something that I can at least try to understand.

Empirically anyway, the quarterbacks and receivers
adhering as best as they can to their precocious signals,
several unspoken or otherwise numerical,
about when to swerve or not between the shrubbery
in their self-contained unit of asphalt.
With driveway end zones and sidewalk out-of-bounds
and the momentary disruptions for passing traffic,
of course, being spent arguing over the rules
or the degree of reciprocity for their most recent failure
with no side willing to take the blame for a slant-cut
being confused with a down-and-in
and another pass play gone awry.

But they dust themselves off and huddle-up
to try again, hoping this time to get it right,

and begin professing once more
before becoming either trusting or gullible
when smashing into the line,
as if faith can be somehow learned.

Not Wanting to Say Good-bye

That whimsical smell of autumn
still lingers in the air,
so unmistakable,
yet so eerily non-descript,

disseminating perhaps
from the factory dregs,
from those rusted-out hollows
along the interstate,

perhaps those fire-eaten kilns
held one last puff,
just one last vestige
to be erased;

or perhaps it's the smoky remains
from some old sports page,
now yesterday's news,
of touchdowns and battles won;

or perhaps it's those youthful glances,
wind-swept and being whisked away
like second chances, desperately seeking
one last bastion from where to perch;

or perhaps it's just someone burning leaves
and that smell is those irretrievable and
unfulfilled dreams, but most probably it's
not wanting to say good-bye.

Lilies in the Snow

The question is a frozen breath
through a wrought iron gate,
the question is an inconspicuous
little town.
The question is a solitary man
outlined in January gray,
the question is a weathered stone
covered in so much quiet.

The question is why?
and unresolved pain,
and when? and where? and what?
The question is snow-covered branches
twisting and turning
into answers,
perfectly imperfect,
like some great work of art.

Talking About Golf

I would try to visit my parents every week, for Sunday
dinners. It was a chance to converse with my mom
about son and mother things, and to talk to my father
about baseball or football, whichever was in season,
and furnaces and tomatoes and automobiles; but mostly,
we would talk about golf. Oh, how he loved that game.
Even in the dead of winter being as excited as a schoolboy
when showing me his latest addition to the collection of clubs
he kept in the basement where we would practice our swings,
so effortlessly, before he was diagnosed with cancer.

Several years have now passed since the day
my father called me on the phone:
"I can't golf anymore," he said,
"I just can't make the swing,"
while deep down inside I was actually praying
of course you can, you're my father, you can do anything
as I began foolishly recounting a story
that he had first relayed to me about a wayward
professional golfer, (at the time I couldn't remember his name,)
who, after seeking his father's advice, had once again found
his game – by slowing everything down. "His name was
Bert Yancey," my father said, "But you don't understand,"
then he told me how he had lost his balance during a swing
while attempting to play one last round with his friends.
I tried to sound encouraging but, looking back,
he had called to tell me that he was dying –

and when he said, "Keep your eye on the ball" and
"Remember to hit 'em straight," I think I know now
what he was really talking about.

And when I next visit his grave, I'm sure that,
among other things, we'll be talking about golf.

About You

My mother gave me a poem to read
that she had found in the local newspaper
obituaries, titled "A Mother's Farewell;"
instructions really, about how not to grieve
and not ever having to be alone
even when that day comes for her,
someone always being there to welcome you home.

My mother, once again, thinking of others,
preparing well in advance
as is always the case,
very much before-hand,
to comfort us, even after she's gone.

But mother,
before there is such a poem written
about you, another one begins
and it goes something like this:
Some of the kindest words ever thought
or spoken, though not always heard,
so many times *from* you, about others.
But, my darling mother, who gives so much,
these beautiful thoughts are more times
about you, many times from others,
but so many more times
from me.

Moon River

Hanging on my basement wall
is a small rectangular picture, enclosed
in a 9x15 inch wooden frame, a drawing
of a bald eagle holding in its' beak a banner
with the words "America Forever – 1918,"
perched on top of Old Glory. An heirloom,
passed down through four generations, lastly,
from my father to me. The glass encasing, at times,
captures my reflection as I'm walking by.

If I had known it was going to be the only perfect day
that I would ever have, I would have committed more to
memory. But, unfortunately, I am not one of those who can
remember when three, tying a shoe or blowing out a candle.

Instead, I was seven, perhaps even eight, in the front yard on
a beautiful Saturday morning, crisp and clean, with our crab-
apple tree ready to burst wide open. I was bouncing a rubber-
ball off of the stoop, sometimes the front door, then over the
roof, and riding my bicycle down the driveway and then up
again, all the while my parents busy with their spring cleaning.

While my father was in the backyard cleaning the windows,
I went inside and it smelled like lemons where my mother had
whirled around from room to room romantically dusting to the
songs of Andy Williams. However, my most vivid memory of
that day is actually, a single moment:

I was sitting on my bike at the bottom of the drive watching
my parents, both at the same time, *framed* in happiness.
My father through the breezeway in his white T-shirt and blue
jeans with the backdrop of the world's greenest grass, while
my mother at that very instant was captured singing in the
kitchen window, one of her all-time favorite songs.

Artistic License

Looking back,
forlornly toward the ocean,
with her sandy blonde hair still neatly folded
though being gently stirred by a late afternoon breeze.

With the day complete,
carrying a sea-horse beach pail now empty
except for her dreams of returning one day
to Betsy Cameron's white-border world,
where her waving summer dress
will remain forever in sharp contrast
to the bluish-gray skies,
infinitely cloudy and overcast,
when inside of *There's Always Tomorrow*;

with the irony of the title making the beauty
more sweet, and the agony
more profound.

Lines of Scrimmage

It was in that blustery quadrilateral
where he would nestle his beat-up book bag
close to his chest, before zigzagging in slow motion,
imitating his gridiron heroes.

High-stepping through the would-be defenders
and past those imaginary yard-line markers
that he knew would one day become blurred
with those futuristic and gladly forfeited lines
of scrimmage. Yet, straining with every fiber
to somehow forgo that "dog eat dog" of growing old
and praying for time, like that December, to freeze

right there,

between those individual houses
and the familiar streets,
or in that farther alleyway
alongside the apartment buildings
and the ten-mile creek
thus, no longer having to walk to school;

but able to turn around
and walk back to that comfy old house
on Bradmore.

Heroes of September

Having to teach during that upcoming week, once more,
the branches of our democratic government, as the painted
leaves begin to ticker-tape from the trees, reminding us to
remember. They tumble, like a mystical tin of used-up crayons
being spilt haphazardly onto one enormous table by some
didactic giant, the colors becoming ever more distant outside
these empty lines of harvested field.

But will it ever feel the same? The anniversary is on the
eleventh, but for me, also the sixteenth, when again I can hear
the roar of a distant crowd; of touchdowns, still one of my
most favorite things on any given Saturday, or Sunday,
as the leaves continue to tumble and fall.

Having to teach during that upcoming week, once more,
following the origin of our language from the Phoenicians
to the Greeks, our Western Heritage, or rotation and
revolution – though the spinning axis not quite the same
and uncontrollable at times, still regretting not having shared
just one last afternoon of watching football with my dad.

Due Diligence on the Seventeenth

The air felt strange
that very next morning
with everyday *laissez-faire* coming into focus;
the dew becoming individual droplets
on single blades of bent grass.

Their moisture poised and patiently hanging
as the universe suddenly became more expansive,
the clouds now moving faster
with the world having been unhinged.

Beneath the bluest blues
and whitest whites,
there was a crisp taste biting
in that splendiferous chill of autumn
and with those over-lapping rows
came a peculiar tingling of the senses.

Mowing thorough,
the way he would have done,
paying attention to detail, well-disciplined,
making sure to complete the task
no matter how difficult;
for there still remained only one way to do things –
the right way,
never *"half-assed."*

Now those harvested seeds may begin to scatter
but that westerly-wind is blowing strangely familiar
and I'm thinking once more about those things
that I must do.

Making Love

I made my sense of what you said, but only later,
about making love, about finding the time,
when we're setting alarm clocks and making sandwiches,
when we're blowing our kisses, instead of kissing good-bye.

But I say love is that bread on the table,
love is that weariness at the end of the day,
love is like a soft breath on a winter's window,
love is knowing what to expect and where to stay.

Tonight we'll lie with the darkness all around us,
in the coolness, I'll feel your warm breath upon my arm,
in the silence, like a fog, I'll begin dreaming,
then endlessly searching for my way back home.

For love is when you find that place where you belong
and love is then doing what must be done,
for love is more work than it is math or science
and love isn't just measured after each setting sun.

So those with castles, my dear, may still have nothing,
and those with something, have something to lose,
and though we have yet to answer all of life's questions,
please know, that I'm always making love with you.

Diane

You were the smoke
rising at the end
of that cold, raw day,
you were the horizon
down that long dirt road
and that most beautiful
of all sunsets.

You were in the night-time sky
when reaching for that farthest
most unattainable star,
you were my dreams
never realized,
all of the planets
and all of their moons.

You were my imagination
when wanting
to begin again,
you were my destination
when finally through,
and now
you are my universe,

but always, it was you.

II. THE SCHOOLHOUSE

The Schoolhouse

Loving the past is like kissing a ghost,
a beautiful visage
as it slowly disappears.

Forgotten, but for the morning blanket
of January snow, an enchanting but bedraggled place,
where this small town's yesterdays must have gone,

and there was this curious feeling of innocence
that went tingling through to my fingertips when, on tiptoes,
I slightly tilted toward one of the frosted panes

to swirl and peer through the milky-white glass
and then like an artist's brush put back in its' stand
just leaned there and wondered,

what life must have been like back then? For the
teachers and students with those reciprocating stares, with their
memories now scattered amongst the broken wooden chairs

strewn, as if for firewood, but looking like
a stick figure square dance frozen in mid-step,
with a weather-beaten plaque outside

left only partially reading:
ONE ROOM – IN 1892,
while I watched my footprints begin to fade

and then disappear,
as I slowly became one of them
with our kindred spirits whispering, "I was once here."

Some Days

> *Cogito, ergo sum.*
> *(I think, therefore I am.)*
>   - Rene' Descartes (1637)

Nothingness woke me again,
can't shut it off.
For this I should be thankful?
Abject, stark, cold,
curse Descartes
and Darwin
and Job
and myself,
knowing one has to be right;
and jealousy
and discrimination
but mostly equality,
for they lied to us you know,
because it's equity
and empathy
and I am here.
Can't you see me?
Oh, if only you could.
But, perception is what you *think* you see,
for I am under here –
under this crushing weight
of being.

Having Never Been to Idaho

For those who have never shoveled,
who have never awakened to a dream,
to a frozen ocean of silent white
and all of those drifting waves

and to gray clouds slowly becoming
anything they want,
but looking so decent and honorable
after giving you all that they've got

and to a suddenly foreign landscape,
now a beginning without an end,
and somehow reminiscent of Idaho
though I have never actually been

and to a furrowed brow and to the clenching of fists
and to thinking *I'm still here you bastards*, before again
slipping into the breach
to search for that tremendous feeling of accomplishment

when with those mountains and valleys complete
and with that rugged western-look upon your face
becoming the Marlboro Man with your breath slowly rising
while imagining Wyoming and riding the fences

and just to be left standing alone
in that vast piece of nothing,
colored in a magnificently pale shade
of forgotten.

Winter Birds

Just a dark smudge through the bedroom window,
at first, that went sweeping across the parchment sky,
hanging and then darting through the grayness,
a kind of scripture being written from on high

before exploding into a rarefied confetti,
February fireworks that wouldn't fall to the ground,
instead inventing their own kind of circus
landing like trapeze artists upon a single wire

where they perched in a high rent district,
these country club wives sitting side by side,
squawking back and forth about the latest gossip
and ruffling each others' feathers without really trying

until a shimmering string of black pearls,
that for a single moment I held in my hand,
but the reception line kept growing longer
with those waiting to park, circling overhead.

Muirfield

Our little piece of mortgaged earth,
through deaths and weddings
and most recently a neighbor's birth,
having moved from Toledo
to this street with a Scottish name

and bordering another
with a DEAD END sign
in bold black letters,
with a backdrop like sunshine,
yellow and cracking

and lifting,
like this dead gray face of winter,
exposing a museum of artifacts,
mostly old beer bottle caps
and tiny strings of blue ribbon

and these curious pieces of paper
making friends with last years leaves
with memories of Christmas and birthdays
while laying amongst the slumbering grasses
of brown and green

and as our two favorite geese
heading for the northeast
honk a "good-morning"
as they pass by,

we're content to stay right here
slowly raking up the preceding year,
while having an intimate conversation
between just husband and wife.

Morning Drive

Life can slip by unnoticed,
as another day is brushed lightly upon the eastern sky,
yet there are certain moments that randomly take a hold of you,
as I watched a homeless women slowly waving at
the passers by:

What a chore it must be to be in her world
of emptiness and awkward smiles,
with all of these driveways and sidewalks
and alleyways and streets, it's so much colder here
when there's no one by your side;

then as the sun began to sift through the trees
a "Jesus fish" shone in front of me,
with a broken fin,
on a banged-up blue trunk lid,
with a bumper sticker reading, "Luke, Chapter 23;"

as a young girl played at a bus stop
spinning in circles with her face toward the clouds,
impatiently waiting for her destiny in a plaid matching skirt,
though forever losing those precious seconds
with every time she went around.

American Teacher

Not dedicated to my many wonderful students –
you know who you are.

"Some old bald dude," that was it, the entirety of his thought, a first day student standing outside of my classroom when describing me to his friends. A young man with a tattooed neck who just didn't seem to care, that I had once had long strawberry-blonde hair and was said to have run like the wind.

Perhaps it was because my tongue wasn't pierced that he didn't seem to care, that hundreds of insufferable ingrates like him were still reverberating inside the corridors of my head:

"Get out my grill home boy."
"Why you all up in it?"
"Who you baby daddy is?"
"Man, you be trippin'."

Thirty years of uneducated drivel from teenagers who know it all, except for courtesy and respect and to hike up their pants and to sometimes listen, rather than talk.

"Some old bald dude," that was it, for what could he possibly learn from me, this grizzled veteran with no spring in his step nor a song left in his heart? Just a beat-up punching bag with nothing to give sitting stoically in his chair, y*et with his mind still racing for miles and miles ... so comfortably, and way ahead.*

Still Thinking of Cezanne

A painter with eyesight failing,
his once incredible use of light
reduced to a checkerboard of dramatic shadows,
with images less defined
though colors more defiant,
his earthy umbers and daunting ocher
now something else entirely;
post-impressionistic cubism,
absolutely brilliant.

A metamorphosis through the dying years
and once more lifting the human spirit,
but this time, by stacking bricks.

Still thinking of Cezanne,
this French provincial
and largely forgotten man,
and how he saved his best for last,
faithfully creating his most inspiring works
when blind, using mostly
the hand of God.

Raising the Kursk

A love letter, wrapped in a hopeful water-proof plastic,
written in an icy cold desperate blackness, a lonely Russian
good-bye from the bottom of the Bering Sea. Listing some

of the one-hundred and eighteen inhabitants, all of whom
inhaling their last breaths, and saying *I love you* among some
hurried other things and then ending with – *do not despair.*

Intended to softly pierce Olga's heart just one last time,
married only six months, his beautiful eastern European bride
incredulously waiting for her heroic sailor poet to come home

in this sunken nuclear coffin, towed into port one year too late,
with his distraught widow still in disbelief, *"I can't imagine
how he found the strength – to write those amazing words."*

The Artistry of Gehry

Little squiggles,
magically becoming
awe-inspiring buildings,
the strange and wonderful sketches
of a modernistic visionary.

Sculpted in concrete, or glass, or steel,
with his architectural anomalies sometimes looking
like the breasts of an odd California woman.
And whether finding inspiration from a garbage can
or believing that decoration is a sin
his designs have been described
as a transcendental state
with the Gugenheim of Bilbao
having become his cathedral.

One of his creations now stands
only a few miles from where I live,
adjacent to the Toledo Museum of Art,
having been compared to a castle of the Renaissance
or even an ocean-fairing freighter
having already navigated the Great Lakes
and now safely docked at port.

Waiting in Line with the Missing Link

I knew I had seen that face before,
petrified in a history book, a hominid skull,
lying for seven million years
in the southern Sahara.

Now plastered upon
this distinguished-looking gentleman,
unable to move, standing in front of me,
after asking a yellow-coated lady
if this was the very best
that she could do.

Saying phrases like "wicked googly"
and "stuck in a sticky wicket,"
while being swallowed alive
by the Detroit Metropolitan Airport
and all the while still trying to impress upon the attendants
to somehow, make the line move faster.

But after politely refusing to ask any more questions
and with his breaking point having been reached,
he turned around and in the most profoundly human way,
was expressionless.

The Deconstruction of Les Robertson

An apology,
to the structural engineer of the Twin Towers.

Mortar
and brick
and mortar and brick,
building a reputation from
the bottom up – of course, a lifetime
of work to instantly debunk, this *everyone*
knows how to do. It always being easier to throw stones,

to rip apart, to destroy rather than build, for the job of any
critic is to critique that which is transparent,
translucent or opaque – governmental
red-tape, the collective conscience
now being cleansed at
the expense of his
good name.

So richly
deserved, yet
reduced to a whisper – when
asked to apologize for something
of which he was not to blame, though
remorseful each day, knowing full-well the imperfections
of mankind and himself, and once more, building with bricks.

The Hotel Victory

Named for Commodore Oliver Hazard Perry
when he captured the British, almost single-handedly,
at The Battle of Lake Erie
in eighteen-thirteen;

the largest and most majestic hotel in the world,
a multi-towered Queen Anne-styled structure,
built with mules in three years and then opened
in eighteen-ninety-two.

So forty-four miles east of Toledo
by upper-class sloop and passenger steamer
they came to South Bass Island and legendary
Put-in-Bay;

but of the multitudes of tourists,
from their skiffs and their schooners,
who raise their glasses in the downtown taverns
each year,

only a few will salute the flag by the cannon
and fewer yet will sift through the forgotten grandeur
from that devastating fire
in nineteen-nineteen.

Dempsey vs. Willard

The heavyweight championship fight for the world,
July 4, 1919, at Bay View Park in Toledo, Ohio.

In un-Godly heat, well over one-hundred degrees,
with the sap from the make-shift split-rails oozing
causing many a gent to lose his britches
and cover himself with newspaper while wandering around
the half-filled and hastily built eight-thousand seat stadium

with the famous western lawman Bat Masterson collecting
weaponry at the gate, guns and knives, to avoid any
shenanigans or mishaps like drunkards bathing in the barrels
of lemonade and thus ruining the lot for the folks getting hotter

with the fight ready to begin and with "The Manassa Mauler,"
like a ferocious cat, pouncing on the enormous Willard
from the opening bell and knocking him down five times,
then being carried off by a frenzied and jubilant mob
only having to return in the nick of time

with the threat of disqualification, for the referee
having never officially surrendered the match
to the chagrin of Dempsey's manager
who wagered most of his life's savings
on a first-round knock-out, but

with the second and third just a formality
for the beaten and battered Willard,
his face now grotesquely disfigured,
having been pummeled into relenting submission

with five missing teeth and a broken jaw
and several cracked ribs,
the vanquished giant
quietly boarded a train for home.

Huron Avenue

HEATED PIANO ROOMS
and other ghostly and forgotten words
are slowly fading into the brick
of a downtown building.

In sketchy white and transparent paint,
once neatly printed, now becoming more faint
with each passing moment,
like a melancholy dream:

of streetcars and spiral towers,
gray fedoras and buttoned collars,
and horse-drawn carriages
through the rising steam.

There's abandoned alleys and lofty views
with a few new restaurants, but still empty rooms,
just some bells and whistles
with the distant clattering of hooves.

III. TIGER STADIUM

Tiger Stadium

Everything is the past,
for what is, is no more,
and the future is yet to be.

Everything seemed green back then and cold
to the little boy at his first football game
sitting next to his dad. Surrounded by,
and inundated with, the indelible smells
of cheap-ass cigar smoke and so many spilt beers
while watching the numbers change on the
gigantic black board above the bleachers,
showing all the other scores, from all the other games,
in all the other cities. And *he* was in Detroit!
He was actually there, sitting next to his dad.
The Lions won that day and he was so alive,
and so in love, with everything.

Everything had turned blue by then as the young man
was sitting in the sun watching his umpteenth baseball
game surrounded by his childhood friend. Yes, this stadium
was his everything! It was as if he could take the whole
place into the palms of his hands, give it a good shake,
and make it fake snow. He knew every entrance,
he knew every exit, he knew every square inch,
he was in total control. That was until some years ago,
when they suddenly closed the doors – forever.

Everything was white there in his dream
where his stadium now laid in ruins. A painful reminder
of what used to be, barely recognizable, but he knew what
it was. There was a partial shell with some pillars and posts

that had somehow moved to Toledo and stood next to his
childhood home. And as he encircled the catacombs of the
tunnels and the sarcophagus of the right-field stands,
at first, he couldn't seem to find a way in, and then,
he couldn't seem to find a way out. And all he really
knew for sure, was that, the little boy was lost.

Something Genuine

We noticed each other
from across the street
as I was walking by,
a moment of indecision.
She was water-soaked, maybe four,
wearing a purple bathing suit
while adorning the sprinkler on her front lawn.

We shared an instant of self-consciousness,
I don't have a place to hide,
then she un-crisscrossed her hands
that were covering her knobby little knees
and gave the most unpretentious smile.

Then we smiled at each other
and waved good-bye
and she went running back through the spray;
then she turned one more time,
her body half-way around,
and then she went running again.

April Morning

It begins, ever so slowly,
as just a sliver and then a vernal slice
of a burgeoning orange florescence – then gradually
taking all of this, provincial insignificance, and making it
come alive. So beautiful, that I am occasionally unable
to pull myself away from the rectangular warmth of our
picture window, as the early light creeps and crawls
until framing my bare feet on the living room floor.

It begins, with the plum blossoms in full bloom,
like precious puffs of pink smoke,
and with the opposing hydrangea of white, pink, and blue,
and with the neighborhood children brushing-by
as if an impressionistic painting,
on their way to school like hurried little dabs
of indiscriminate red, yellow, and blue,
and sometimes green, with the tiniest voice
coming from somewhere in between shouting
"wait for me," with an un-tucked shirttail of white
flapping in the breeze, like a lonely cloud,
scurrying through the mercurial sky,
in search of a friend.

Though now, it looks as if,
it almost wants to rain.

Wamba Road

When the world slows
and the wind softly blows
and all is right
for a while,
and the bad dreams go away
up into the heavens
and we can breathe
and smile,
knowing we have faith
once more,
in what we believe.

There are times, that remain,
though closely guarded secrets
and of only certain things
being told by the air
or through the trees
in the early-morning light
before vanishing,
amongst the roaring crowd
of summer's wavering iridescence,
but then from somewhere in the distance
there's the incense of old newspapers
and grandma's kielbasa.

And for a moment,
the pastel Virgin Mary
is watching over us again
and we are safe in grandpa's backyard
with watermelon and whiffleball,
playing in that wispy smoke
as it emanates and slowly rises

from the charred barrel behind the garage,
and forever searching in the high grass and wildflowers,
through the spider webs and rotten apples,
for our most prodigious home runs –
but then, I am unable to recall
just where the apple tree had stood.

A mere flicker,
when one feels whole.

Phantom Moon

Two o'clock in the morning,
southern Michigan, a "No-Man's Land,"
with the distant flashes of light, silent harbingers;
for the rumbling and the cracking
and the zigzagging to the ground,
the electricity from the heavens
joined together, arm in arm,
dancing like wild Russians
with those booming sounds,
like an enemy howitzer burning red,
punching holes into the darkness
and shaking the earth
until dawn.

But that July morning carried with it,
along with the sun's familiar face,
an eerie orange-ness from a daytime moon,
hanging low in the western sky,
with the warm circle of the barrel's end
still glowing.

Vacationing in Au Train

In the upper part
of the Upper Peninsula,
just a few miles down the road
from Christmas, Michigan,
where the black bears would forage
near that quiet little inlet
called Harrington's.

In the coolness of the moonlight,
puttering the one-prop through the rising mist,
swish-swooshing across the darkened waters
to find the yellow-striped perch,
or into the whistles of those lonely reeds
for that one largest of small-mouthed bass
and in the meanwhile on that painterly surface
with those far-away sounds
of mostly silence.

My Photograph

Just a simple image
on standard paper
yet I find myself
once more,
back in that glorious sunshine
of another time
and back in the backwoods
of Au Train.

With camera in hand,
viewing my younger brother,
six years old,
like it was yesterday,
perfectly-centered,
with his raccoon cap
and homemade shillelagh;
snap!

And there it is,
hanging on my dining room wall
to this very day.

So now,
and every now and again,
he's still walking behind
and in-between
our mom and dad,
down that long dirt road.

The Beach

An old pocket-watch lies hidden
beneath some frills in the top drawer,
though sometimes in secret
is still being held to her ear,
as if it were a sea-shell,

hoping and wishing to magically hear
from someone who no longer holds time,
with these frozen hands that no longer care

about the measured sands through an hour-glass,
the once shifting grains along the water's edge,
or even of their long ago castles

but, is still trying to hear
something, *if just anything*,
other than the gentle beating
of her broken heart.

Woodlawn

Down at the end of the street
there's a metal-framed canopy under the trees
and there will be the subsequent stirring,
where the webs are like frosting covering the cocoons
enticing young ones to search for the secret passage

and where people will come together once more
for something that shouldn't have happened
and wear pins on lapels and fold triangular flags
and give respects from a grateful nation

and where a fragrantly dry scent will whisk now and then
through the freshly-mowed August grass
and a deafening numbness will be left twisting in the wind
of hyperbole, and muffled syllables

and where a mother will stand outside of herself
while a train's whistle moans in the distance
and children will dare but only sometimes escape
the sensation of a stinging bee.

Bob and Shelly

Our gregarious neighbors
with that *one* house,
where cars are always parked
for main events; like holidays,
or a Tuesday.

With their dogs
Zeus and Shmoo,
the one named after a God
a tiny little thing with a Napoleon complex,

whether strutting around
in his "Bitches Love Me" muscle shirt
at the annual luau

or for hours at a time
sitting in the middle of a neighbor's drive,
then growling

under his doggie breath
when walking away,
after leaving a little pee

and just daring someone
to wear a Bonaparte costume,
come Halloween.

First Day of School

Watching the children
traipsing their way to school
with their dejected little hearts
becoming incrementally heavier,
with each additional step
toward Larchmont
elementary.

From across the street
trying to distinguish between
their indiscriminate sadness
by non-quantifiable degrees,
with their individual voices
so softly speaking
of their lost summer.

No longer floating
as they had in the spring,
not their mostly-empty book bags
nor the slightly-deciduous leaves,
just their little souls escaping
wanting desperately
to be free.

The Disciple

Just listen to the rain
as it dances on the roof,
so softly from heaven
these tiny drops of proof.

My Grandmother used to say that God was sad
when it was raining outside. That it was because
of how people had been misbehaving, or even worse
if there was thunder and lightning.

Yet, somehow knowing
that it could not have been us,
her mischievous angels,
the cause of this great pain,
while faithfully saying her rosary
with knuckles turned-white
and trying to ease the suffering
with every gentle thrust
of her rocking-chair

swoosh,
swoosh,
swoosh,

which slowly became the rhythm
of my own beating heart
as I awakened from a dream of her
and with the skies still dark,
just laid there and listened
to the morning rain.

The Lark

Monday morning, mid-October,
and our meadow is silent,
as silent as my heart;

but for the slightest humming of a wayward bee,
the occasional chirping of a lonely cricket, the
intermittent croaking of a stubborn frog,

for the sun, having been seduced by the wind
and captured by the clouds
has disappeared

and as the swaying branches of the trees outstretch,
with their outlined bodies leaning heavily against this graying
day, their pleading arms are empty,

as empty as my soul, with only
the hint of a distant smoke,
where you once were.

Bogey

My dog likes to chase leaves.

The omnipotent puppy,
in his scruffy little world
of backyard green make believe,
pounces upon his prey
and with fervent joy
shakes his new toy
furiously,
from side to side,
before bounding about
showing-off his latest prize
of yellowish-orange
or purplish-pink
to heap upon
his collection of colors
already captured;
with his brown and white ears
flopping all around,
as he runs
and darts
and dips
and flips
and rolls
and scratches
and snorts
and sniffs
and tinkles
and toodles

and howls
and growls
and gnarls
and barks
and then …
scampers some more,
with his tail wagging
all the while
saluting,
his ever-growing piles.

November's Eve

*"I tell myself, don't walk like an old man,
stand up straight – then I fall down."*
- Fr. James Auth (2010)

Through the turquoise skies and flickering shadows,
amidst the scarecrows and jack-o-lanterns,
on the front porch sitting alone
but for a withered-up potted plant,

watching for each miniature specter
and patiently waiting for my turn,
like a rusty old bicycle leaned against a tree
off the beaten path.

A lone witness to the day's ending
with the sun a mere candle in the wind
reflecting but the faintest of an horizon
as if softly glowing next to one's bed,

but enjoying the beauty of that final moment
when my breath snuffs out the remaining light
and wanting for nothing just being in that
last incredible crispness of October.

My Love

Sometimes, I feel hollow inside,
like a straw, when you and I are not

reading from the same page,
nor thinking the same thoughts,
nor being as one,

when all of my insides are gone,
as if my heart has been
sucked out.

Yes, when you have taken my heart
and put it away, in a secret place no doubt,
perhaps on a shelf behind some books or
hidden in a desktop drawer, but somewhere
in which I haven't thought to look
inside this very house.

Yes, somewhere indeed
that you alone know
safely tucked and locked,

so only you can decide
when to once more
turn the key

and once again,
fill me.

IV. HARWELL'S VOICE

Harwell's Voice

Some things cherished
and ultimately lost
are then cherished
all the more.

One o'clock in the morning
and a staticky voice from the west coast
crackles on the transistor radio
tucked beneath my pillow.
Ernie, my old friend,
speaks to me once more
and forever in my mind.

The sweet sound of spring,
born of magnolia trees
and a southern breeze,
whispers through the years
and through my window
and drifts out into the tranquil backyards of Toledo
and wherever else the flagship sails
to gently rustle the summer leaves
now turning like pages slightly brown.

And though I am quite sure
that I will pay for this tomorrow,
for now it's the last inning
and we're winning,
hanging by a thread,
and the keystone
Trammell and Whitaker
will turn once more
and forever in my mind.

Good-night old friend,
click!

Spy's Carry-out

for Grandpa Harry

We would walk slowly down Wamba,
down that sleepy and gravelly street,
through the streaky soft sunlight
and countless shades of dark green.
Though *more* slowly now,
for grandpa was falling behind
even before we would reach the corner
for one of his very last times,
while the rest of the world
went rushing by.

We would cross at the corner
onto busy Nebraska Avenue
where grandpa could barely make his way,
though trying his best not to show any discomfort
when one of his youthful protagonists
would invariably say, "Come on, just one more block,"
before we could come back, selfishly,
into the shade, retracing our steps
with popcorn and Pepsi-Cola,
never realizing his pain.

And now as I walk my mind
down those *Kuschwantz* streets,
it's like sneaking inside of an old Polaroid picture
of how it used to be,
to that run-down store
with the squeaky wooden floors
and to the grocer
with the shortened Polish surname.

Ode to Toledo

The future great city of the world.
                    - Jesup W. Scott (1868)

From the library rooftop looking down,
as I watch the disappearing sunlight
crawl upon the faded brick of the city,
like a mother's hand
caressing the cheek of her sleepy child,
and listen to the tempestuous winds
howl down the empty avenues,
like a pack of hungry wolves
wailing at the moon,
and feel the darkening clouds as they gather
and envelop the city's once famous structures,
like so many gigantic balloons
having been freed
from their Thanksgiving Day tethers
and wandering aimlessly –
one lone building
whose future now is in the past
glistens in the distance.

One lone building,
made of simple red brick,
amidst the desolate parking lots and alleyways,
boarded-up in an unknown tint of green.

One lone building,
standing in the shadows,
being dwarfed by the remnants of Libbey and Owens and Ford,
with a heart still barely beating.

One lone building,
looking so painfully beautifully
and so desperately alone,
aches my very soul.

Irene

She sits waiting on her barstool with cigarette in hand
and peers out into the night at what used to be
her city, now strangers to one another.

She sits waiting in the darkness, in the shadow of her youth
for the suitor who never comes, who never magically appears
through the wispy clouds of her freshly-puffed Pall-Mall
though lurking around every corner of time and place,
so she waits.

She sits waiting like her city, once so cavalier,
and speaks of downtown and the Tiedtke's Building,
of Swayne Field and the Mud Hens, of Willys-Overland
and the Jeep, of cherry blossoms in the spring
and her mother's backyard; she speaks of anything
to anybody willing to listen, while she sits

waiting,
waiting,
waiting,

for the sealed envelope,
for the loved one's ear,
for the kiss good-bye.

Alex

He would mostly look away, when shy,
as he went plopping down the hallway with his classmates,
considered the broken eggs of society.

But on one snowy December day,
with his thick black belt synched high above his waist,
this slow-witted Santa with the overflowing heart
began delivering to everyone
a morning smile.

Or to the unsuspecting teacher
a playful hug, though he has never done so to me,
rather he simply punches my fist or gives me a thumbs-up
and makes each day a little brighter
with his sunshine, like yoke,
coming from within.

Aaron

Hushed tones
now are used
when speaking your name,
softer than the rest,
in this most awkward place
of intermittent whisper.
Thought somehow different
are you;
an uneasy peace.

The embattled prisoner,
yet again,
for having chosen
when.

Victoria

Third seat,
by the window,
behind Corey.
She sometimes gets her foot caught
in his desk;
don't ask how.

She says the most darling things,
when the room is quiet,
out of the blue:
"I got my shoestrings caught in an escalator once."
"I'm going to be sixteen years old in eight months."
"I like butter."

Such a sweet child.
Such a sweet child.

Paper Boy

Wearing a baseball cap
and blue jeans, riding
a non-descript bicycle,
though not a ten-speed,
he stirs a momentary ripple
down this lonely summertime street.

From his shoulder hangs
an old-time satchel,
throwing from his hip
like with a cowboy's lasso,
he shoots with confidence
through the lazy afternoon air.

Deftly negotiating
every nuance and crevice,
while riding over curbs
and in-between branches,
for his young heart
having not yet been broken.

Little Girl

A solitary figure
walking home from school,
the road less traveled.

Everyday,
I see her play,
her own partner,

talking and twirling
in her isolated little world
of make believe.

She's adorable when it rains,
red raincoat and umbrella,
her yellow boots splashing puddles,

so precious,
so precocious,
so beautiful.

Stay young
little one,
and please don't be alone.

The Funeral Home

Yellow lines
crisscross the blacktop
where children like to play,
where the foul balls
and home runs
are cursed,
and chased,
as they continue to roll
like marbles on the sidewalk,
against their young pursuers' wishes
and in spite of their thrown mitts,
and where there is recent moisture
of sweat and spit,
whenever cars are not parked there
for special occasion.

The Scent

Just a hint, at first,
as you enter their perfect little world
slightly tilting one's head
hoping to delineate the aroma
of miniature desks and cloak rooms,
of finger paints and wooden blocks,
of sleeping mats and Lincoln logs,
of Elmer's glue and the abacus,
of kitchenettes and Crayolas,
(the sixty-four pack,)
of cookies and milk,
and then, gradually,
the aroma becomes …
happiness;

of you,
of a long ago you.

Serendipity

There's something about
a summer night's breeze,
the gentle persuasion
of dancing winds
playing with daylight's final
shadowy silhouette,
fragrantly sweet
and sprinkled with magic
for which you long
to scoop-up
and run,
far away.

The Old Neighborhood

He returns,
each step becoming more comfortable
like a pair of fading blue jeans,
surrounded by working-class porches
and shutters,
their weariness imperceptible through the darkness,
having been masked with earthy emeralds
and auburns,
appearing quite deep and rich
while reflecting the glancing blows of light
being thrown by a punch-drunk moon,
giddy with sentiment and disobeying the darkness,
reuniting their shadows.

And with each additional step
his ease grows,
like a stack of Sunday morning flapjacks,
as the familiar smell of the trees
washes over him like syrup,
sweet and absorbed.

Reunion

Walking to school,
some twenty-odd years late
for the bell.

The terrain was vaguely familiar
resembling some foreign land
once visited,
with nameless markers
for the dead.
And he enjoyed the fact
that he could still dissect the maze,
that he could still navigate its' passage evenly
and without effort,
with every nook and cranny
slowly becoming his own, again;
though the child-sized stairs
now seemed unnatural,
and barely negotiable,
taken one at a time.

Memories

Little gray ghosts
in their ageless world
of the playground.

All at once
so rude,
not to acknowledge one's presence,
yet so kind,
pretending not to notice,
that *someday* has come
and that the best days
and the most cherished years
are now
for only them.

The Playground

Those little gray ghosts
appeared again last night
and whisked through my mind,
past the bicycle rack
and the flagpole
and out to the playground
once more.

And how I desperately
wanted to join them;
though my wistful pleas
went unanswered,
echoing from the walls of my past
to my conspicuous presence,
surrounded only by asphalt,
where we had once
been friends,
standing
all alone.

Diane's Hands

Softer than the petals
of a flower,
softer than a gentle breeze
on a summer's day,
softer than a kiss
(unless she's the one kissing,)
softer than the softest
drop of rain.

Can comfort any sorrow
for her son or her daughter
and ease any worry
for her husband too,
sculpted to perfection,
so elegant and slender,
and the ones that I held
when we both said, "I do."

Used for working and playing
and for praying,
for hellos and good-byes
and for wiping tears,
for hugging and scolding
but mostly for walking,
for I'll be holding one
when we return.

Home

I love my wife because my wife loves me
and because she's my everything and effervescent,
and my wife loves me because I love my wife
though her mother still thinks that she could do better,

and I like my wife because my wife likes me
and because we think alike most of the time,
and my wife likes me because I like my wife
and for some reason she thinks that I'm special,

and I like our house because my wife likes our house
and I love our house because she *really* loves it,
and she says she always has and said she always will
from the very first time that she saw it,

but for the green shutters and the unfinished basement
and the missing porch-rail that have since been altered,
and I like the fact that my wife seems to think
that ours is the best mid-western house in the world,

because it's comfy and cozy with a couch and some chairs
and blankets and pillows and doilies, with a fireplace
in the living room that opens to the kitchen
and I like the fact that my wife decorates early,

for gatherings and holidays and puts up the Christmas tree
but calls it a harvest tree until it's Thanksgiving,
with pumpkins and witches and autumn leaves on the mantle
that turn into candy canes and stockings and Santa,

but I don't like the fact that if it was left up to me
our house would look more like an army barrack,
but I do like the fact that it's not left up to me
because I seriously don't know what I am doing,

and I don't like the fact that my wife seems afraid
of growing old and living with cats, because she doesn't
like cats (or squirrels for that matter) and doesn't
understand why some women adore them,

but I tell her not to worry about growing old
because when I die she can just get a puppy,
and read her books by the fire when it snows or if it rains
and decorate each year for the seasons.